Trigons

Also by John Matthias

Poetry
Bucyrus (1970)
Turns (1975)
Crossing (1979)
Bathory & Lermontov (1980)
Northern Summer (1984)
A Gathering of Ways (1991)
Swimming at Midnight (1995)
Beltane at Aphelion (1995)
Pages: New Poems & Cuttings (2000)
Working Progress, Working Title (2002)
Swell & Variations on the Song of Songs (2003)
New Selected Poems (2004)
Kedging (2007)

Translations
Contemporary Swedish Poetry (1980)
    (with Göran Printz-Påhlson)
Jan Östergren: Rainmaker (1983)
    (with Göran Printz-Påhlson)
The Battle of Kosovo (1987)
    (with Vladeta Vučković)
Three-Toed Gull: Selected Poems of Jesper Svenbro (2003)
    (With Lars-Håkan Svensson)

Editions
23 Modern British Poets (1971)
Introducing David Jones (1980)
David Jones: Man and Poet (1989)
Selected Works of David Jones (1992)
Notre Dame Review: The First Ten Years (2009)
    (with William O'Rourke)

Criticism
Reading Old Friends (1992)

John Matthias

Trigons

Shearsman Books
Exeter

First published in the United Kingdom in 2010 by
Shearsman Books Ltd
58 Velwell Road
Exeter EX4 4LD

www.shearsman.com

ISBN 978-1-84861-125-2
First Edition

Copyright © John Matthias, 2010.

The right of John Matthias to be identified as the author of this work
has been asserted by him in accordance with the
Copyrights, Designs and Patents Act of 1988.
All rights reserved.

Acknowledgements

Although the various sections of this poem are not fully free-standing or independent of context in *Trigons* as a book, the following editors and journals have been generous in committing space to what might have seemed to their readers merely excerpts from an unidentified extended work in progress. I want, therefore, to be specific in saying thanks to the individuals who have been generous to this project during the years of its composition: To Christina Thompson and Don Share at *Harvard Review* (Number 33, 2007) for printing 'Islands, Inlands'; to Herbert Leibowitz and Ben Downing at *Parnassus* (Volume 31, No. 1 & No. 2) for 'Hess / Hess'; to Boris Jardine and Lydia Wilson at *Cambridge Literary Review* (Vol. 1, No.1, Michelmas 2009) for 'Café Des Westens'; to Brian Henry and Andrew Zawacki at *Verse* (Vol. 25, No. 1-3) for 'Roadex Reflex'; and to Carlo Parcelli at *Flashpoint* (Web Issue 12) for 'Aruski Rehab' and 'Chez Harvey Goldberg'.

Contents

Trigon   7

Trigon for an Old War: Three Drafts
    I   Islands, Inlands   11
    II   Hess / Hess   21
    III   Café des Westens Kurfürstendamm   31

Trigon Two: I – III
    Sonnet: Author Note, Revised   43
    Sonnet: Trigon Note, Revised   43

    I   Roadex Reflex   45
    II   Aruski Rehab   61
    III   Chez Harvey Goldberg   77

Coda   93

Sonnet: Send   109
Sonnet: Delete   110

Trigon

(1) Latin: both a ball to play with and a game played by ancient Romans involving three players standing in a triangle. Players caught with the right hand and threw with the left. Cf. Petronius, *Satyricon*, where the *pilecripus*, or score-keeper, does not count the number of times the players successfully pass the ball, but instead the number of balls that drop on the ground. A joke? Or the actual method of scoring? (2) Astrology: three member signs of triplicity and third harmonic, 120 degrees, the most influential major essay aspect; blends planetary energies, harmoniously indicating the ease of expression; a group of three signs belonging to the same element: *Fire* (Aries, Leo, Sagittarius); *Earth* (Taurus, Virgo, Capricorn); *Water* (Cancer, Scorpio, Pisces). (3) D.C. Comics: all-powerful ruler of an alternate dimension who wishes to extend his influence to the Earth. Cf. Mephisto. (4) Music: A three-sided ancient Greek or Roman lyre. A neume of obscure interpretation used in the notation of manuscripts from the Abbey of St. Gall. A German based fusion band characterized by many changes in its line-up and by jamming as a source for their music. (5) Gemology: triangular etch pits seen on natural surfaces of a diamond. (6) Poetics: A set of three poems each in seven sections of varying length. May involve many changes in their line-up and jamming as a source of music. (7) Plural: Logic puzzles published by Dell Magazines and others; title of a book by John Matthias.

(Google dictionaries; OED; Fanciful)

Trigon for an Old War:
Three Drafts

I

Islands, Inlands

1.

Ionian to Middle Sea by caïque ...
Crete, then Cairo ... A long telling of it and
a tilling in a short red boat—
                          And Corcyra,
which may have been the island where *The Tempest*
tossed a crew, may have been before the home of Phaeacians
who to foreigners were kind.
Scheira, Corfu—
where shadow-play Karaghiosis is the hero, Spiridion the saint.
In Paris the pornographer receives a Zero letter in
heraldic hand: *I fear a war is coming on. I love your work.*
So did the diplomat from Smyrna. Love and fear.
Fear the war and love the work.
When consul in Albania.
While following the kingdom come
                                  by caïque on to Crete...

2.

. . . or Corfu first
before they all began to enter one another's tales.
While Karaghiosis raised the dead in shadow-play
to thrill an island's children torches lit
the carbide lamps for men with tridents waiting
in their circles of illumination for the dog's-head eel
and squid. On cat's-back streets they'd cast out Judas
on their Fridays good & bad &
spit black ink or red and yellow feathers
firing pistols in the air and banging pans all bottoms up
and lids with wooden spoons—
       Cacophonous
and fearful as the lights at sea
becoming lights in air
the flare and tracer flash-lit wing and tail of aircraft
that Apollo's maker cast in upward
parabolic fall all down and dawnward pilot splayed
and child's work his wreck
while in their boats the patient fishermen all night

3.

awaited Paraclete! . . . or parachutes that flower from
the bellies of eviscerated
Icari their airman's progeny disgorging over Crete
a sum of all the fathers' fear of suns.

                Spiridion might
yet achieve a miracle
collect his dues upon his saint's day might
yet disembody don'ts by prodding open mouths with
long dildoic finger plucked in shadow-play's
echt Deutsch nicht wahr yon exiled Müller from New York
but only happy in the sun a swim a walk
a milling in exaggeration of colossi talks and talks
a Yank to outflank
all Hellenophiles among the Brits . . .
                              he'd lived
in Montparnasse without a thought
of what the mountain meant. And all the better
For *I love your work*
come hither cousin even if you know less Greek

4.

but more a little Latin like the
General Kreipe's kidnapped from his car by Childe Patrick
and his band Paddy fresh from walks half round
the world Kreipe'd spit black ink like dog's-head squid
himself or songbirds like the Corfu cats
unless a dawn broke over Ida, then
instead his
          Vides ut alte stet
nive candidum soracte
stopped the action for a moment
though a supposition even after mishaps on the road from
military quarters to his villa at Knossos
that he dealt with cretins
Stratis Mitso Nikko and the others helping him
to hurry just a little Horace into
that back seat even if you do lose your Iron Cross
had made his name-in-jest Theophilis
his *Wagan* O an Opal and his captor Paddy's answer to him
nec jam sustineant onus chap I know it well

5.

enough as consul in Albania thirty-six to thirty-eight
becomes a pal of Corfu's brothers in the art that
winter's Indian summer from before the war
Les Anges Sont Blancs he wrote for Brooklyn's Capricornian
and then in Greek about *a sailor in the shrouds*
as island shores begin to look like fish bones
on the sand . . .
                       To all eight points
his blood is scattered in the wind when Mr S. Thalassinos
describes a man—who will till the story of his life?
a bell tolls a traitor equally with patriot may tell—
Seferis's *logos dekapentasyllavos* all given up
for Doric clarity
and eros in demotic and the crotch like half
the Brits he washes up eventually in
Alexandria to fiction faction fornication where the god
abandoned Antony the Yank abandoning
the marriage feast of Harmony & Cadmus for Big Sur
for such is fate Señor and yet
the alphabet was left us when alas ambrosia
turned to *vin ordinaire* and Icor
just to poor plain red & human blood spilled & spilling
in the deserts mountains seas

6.

and islands too, fit for Eucharist in world conflagration
civil war religious strife or song
in the Sixties when they did their torturing in Leros
you would find
not a single Turk among those Greeks who'd
cut the right hand off each other's arm
even as it plucked the instrument
bouzouki or guitar
we listened to in London dancing with the women we
would wed and heard that Lena's father
was arrested by the Junta colonels leaders of the coup &
Theodorakis grim behind glad honor's
dog & cat both buried in the torch-light late at night.
A year before we'd visited the isolato
in a black spring and heavy fog rolling down the hills
above Carmel he said he missed those islands
missed those friends but he was old and even sometimes
weary with a bad back and stiff knee
Britain too an island but as inlanders we danced
a foreign dance in 6/8 time and tried to sing in *laiki phoni*
when we could
the *rembetika* drawing on but stood entirely
still and listened to the *Romancero Gitan*, Lorca Greeked
by Heraklian for descending minor thirds to tonic
clattering beyond Falangist Spain flamenco pistol on the hip
but not complicit with the ringing phone and
Lena weeping so they've taken him to Leros oh my God
her gentle father who
would read to her Elytis and Seferis when she cried

7.

inland from the skull
                    another island where we live
and which we cannot reach
but still it wills love it wills death networked
by rivers of our blood the self's fish
swimming in the circles of illumination made by neural lamps
for trident-fisher's epileptic wish to fly & just
a snip of *corpus callosum*   : :
                    two hemispheres their
two singers two wedding feasts two hallucinated histories
with dances all their own
how Hellenic
Paraclete to come a comforter
from *parakalein* with parables that come
a cropper when the skies
fill with parachutes again at night
and mind's all complicit with the migraine ringing
uncanny the occult of Lesbos
or of Leros
            whose parabiosis then in this our isle?
what saint or hero in the mind Spiridion
Karaghiosis *which* pornographer will leer through Zero
in the fear of love & work when
kingdom comes between us probes like god's
goad electric stimulates *thalassa and thalassa* oceanic
and unhealed washed over
under some tsunami of the mind a thought
thinking selfsame island inland
from the skull a Crete Corfu Leros Lesbos
on by caïque where you will

II

Hess / Hess

1.

          d   nsshe and his   alHof   out and off
as mummery s a much of amory's own
muscle memory of stretched out string or aileron a Messerschmitt
or Steinway Myra saying *what?* as parachute
re-opens Parsifal and paper headlines
Hess Arrives in basement of the National her proof of concept
Russians for the moment fail to get it *Do you let*
and this arriving Cabinet War Room *Do you let*
his wife perform all over England when he's Nazi number two?
a sucking band of burning brands
the orchestra not bad but Queen's Hall too had taken a bad hit
you know those hands must be like steel do
you understand how much the forearms ache how much
the back will almost break to brace
his reputation as an airman Fokker D before his father's firm
in Alexandria expropriated as the work
of aliens beyond the opus 57 was the shelling of Vienna
B hiding in his cousin's basement was this blitz
the Marshals of Napoleon up on the Kahlenberg dropping
shells outside or music

2.

hard to tell the difference with the roar inside your head
if Archduke Rudolph flees the city with
the children who are you to stay the pictures gone
into some cave in Wales and the empty walls like windows on
the *Anschluss* B erects his structure on the tonal pillars
F and A and D extends arpeggiatted sweep to Neapolitan resolve
Napoleonic entry to a point of most remove
and you can pray again for some repeat of winter's tale 1812
some repeat of half-step modulation to a dead dance of frozen bodies
in a tundra where they snap the fingers off
their friends and suck them till they ooze a bit of marrow
for it's cold in the basement cold at 20,000 feet
adrenaline will fire the amygdala strengthen via neural pathways
memory the fingers play the hands fly the Bf110C5
will drop from well above cloud nine to less approximate
sublime your body knows although your conscious mind forgets
to loop the plane before you leap two octaves falling backward
pulling at the stick a half-roll would do it by the book
the D-ring ripcord a diminished-seventh cord and downward
from the dominant to tonic up again by an inversion while I
simply try to type by touch and muck it up as if I'd
ad a sodden stoke ambt ould nt it da keys
but reach for something distant in confusion take a look
yourself at youtube.com/watch?v=UNlyxn2Y4_E
before you read

3.

another word. They'll tell you that's the best first movement
ever played. *Appassionata* even got to Lenin, here
performed by Myra looking like the cleaning lady not like
our contemporary babes who graduate from Juilliard
to make debuts like MTV madonnas on the move
who show a leg and deep breathe to open cleavage all the way
to nipples this machine is not Peter Quince an old clavier
and not my Fifties Olivetti either
if Ms Triple Forte thumps to flood into our right hemisphere
and auditory cortex why not the penis also
pulsing blood. In 1840 Clara Schumann introduced to all Berlin
not only this sonata but the tightrope walk
of playing such a thing without a score a novelty the critics
called "theatrical" but doubtless frightened male virtuoso rivals
right out of their patronage. By heart, by heart we say.
She said she heard the bomb whistling fall directly through
the Renaissance and not detonate her dignity in service
to the music (all German) made to serve as sign that London lived
even underneath that empty gallery Holbein Ambassadors
lost to all diplomacy the Luftwaffe pounding at its very worst
that day the Deputy took methyl benzedrine and atropine
preparing for a long flight
                                        there where you see her
youtube.com watch 1941
and not the girl from Juilliard and not either
Clara Schumann or indeed the cleaning lady or your old
music teacher touching with her fingers

4.

every octave of your fear by heart like missile memory.
I think my wife's got it from her
embryonic state the year the V-2s started and her mother
bump bumped she told me butt-step down by butt-step
into Charing Cross underground a shelter then
so gently gently fearing so
to lose the child. But that was later on. Now the only
movement in the basement is those hands
the small group exhausted but attentive all around her *more*
than attentive *wholly rapt* some of them in raincoats
galoshes one still with his hat on sitting on the floor
and leaning up against the wall because the chairs are occupied
and all but weeping for the gift of this while in another
basement sandbagged at doorway facing St. James Park
and Horseguards Road Captain Adams soon to be the father
of the woman looking now above my shoulder
at my hands & M's greets because he's duty officer in May
Attlee Eden Beaverbrook and the P.M. his wife
not yet pregnant plotting movements of the incoming planes
and half east London weeping for this gift.
Closed the window did you know Archambeau I once met
Tambimuttu in the Sixties?—still erotic, still an editor of this
and that who wove his way through blacked-out
streets to find the girls left behind by high fliers in their
spitfires everybody's Tambi who would publish poets blackballed
at *Horizon*. I've told Anania about how he would
hold court in bed his *levée* supervised by sycophants who couldn't
write you know but he could listen even he
could listen even *his* ego

5.

shut down by the music of those hands motor-neuron
network was not up to Messerschmitts
in Spandau Prison where like Tambi he had supervised *levées*
in 1961 when I was in Berlin. We photographed him
walking solitary with *the sun appearing late and disappearing
early without any strength* he told us he'd become a
music critic and philologist who'd liquidate the Y reduce the caps
on nouns as for example *hümne, hüdrant, korgesang*
as better English sing along dear friend goodbye Speer goodbye
my six companions hang yourself for opus 57 if you've
tried to end a war: 17.45 hours G.S.T. and
do you think about your tongue your lips a glottal stop or
sibilant or do you speak do you think about anatomy
the tendons nerves and firing neurons trying to be *gründlich*
fingers how they strike a key forearm weight
or whole arm now & by the poise or balance tone
produced by follow-on in key-descent don't think about it
find the music in the music slipstream pressing you
so hard your body cannot move don't think about it stiffening
just speak you wouldn't theorize the motions of your lips
to kiss your mouth to drink a manual somewhere
nonetheless explains it don't think about it
or the mission or the music poor Wellington is melted
into candle wax but somehow the Emperor
and Marshal Ney are blasted still intact with half-facsimile
of B's pianoforte through the window of Tussaud's
pages from the score of opus 57
rising in the air like other ash she doesn't need it anyway
memo for the press and posters for the town from
Beaverbrook: turn your pots and pans into
Spitfires and Hurricanes your kettles vacuum cleaners
hat pegs and shoe trees bedroom fittings household goods
and ornaments or anything with any little bit
of metal War Office offers five hundred tons of saucepans
Royals said to eat off second best

6.

bed or dine out on entrails of the one who strafed
the Palace although Rudolf Hess will do who has arrived
the paper says the Laureate corrects his line where
mistyped *seeker* nearly goes to press striving in his line
for *a world where every sucker finds the beauty*
and the joy and later in the day writes to Dear Edith Sitwell
though he types in fact *Deaf Edith* notes it and
changes it to *Dead Edith* one's distracted by the bombs
falling all around don't think about it
miss a note a name Napoleon or Wellington who cares
they're only made of wax and bees out
in Grantchester collecting pollen from the May flowers
May ball still celebrated is it with those gaudies
no bombs falling there to turn the Cam
into a fiery lower Thames a musicologist this very moment
in his rooms at Trinity experimenting with the method
of LaRue where P designates a theme in opus 57—*a* then
a phrase and x and y the sub phrases—*Pax* is ar
peggiated main theme and *Pay* the trilled figure following
in aviation *Pax* is the cockpit section of an aircraft
used for training *Pax* in genetics a transcription factor
of the helix-turn-helix nine member proteins
Pax-1 to *Pax-9* but gentlemen and scholars it's a paid-up
spoonerism kind of touch it's just a missed note
and X will mark the spot where duty officer
observes a plane approaching on his way to the Cabinet
War Room walking quickly under Nelson's column and
across the square saying to himself *thermite incendiary*
hydrants working in this zone

7.

hümne and korgesang. The sun approaching late and
disappearing early without any strength would not however well
describe the city in the spring. Spandau winters
yet to come. Yet to come her own lapse on stage when right hand
and left become all dis co
ordinate her foot foot her feet begin
to pedal pedal spasm jerks his neck to snap his spine who wrote
again I lost my memory in cell number seven who could find
a high window latch extension cord & just step off a chair
Ich hab's gewagt he wrote
.*dares* and *did* dare
at last that flight
hymns & chorusing however do not follow by the logic
of a pilot's neuromuscular facilitation
even if you charge
the currents with a max of acetylcholine
drench the synapses depolarize the motor neurons bind receptors
when they finally get the PM more or less
convinced the Deputy has parachuted into Scotland on his own
initiative it's already been a trying day he says *I simply won't*
go and hear that lady play piano in a crypt
officer with flashlight on against all regulations catches
in the beam suspicious lurker some sleeper who was
suddenly awakened when Enigma in his Chelsea attic
turned on decoded R and H – *the lunatic has taken off for Britain*
soon enough to be transported to the villa Mytchett Place
near Aldershot *where sweet wisteria* he writes
and rhododendrons bloom
in all colors and the music room leads into a garden
as it does in Harlaching where every day she plays him opus 57
every day he claps his hands until they sting for he
is só grateful she is só good at playing German music when
the others he has come to save will not
he knows she plays right through the terrible attacks their

fingers move together when he watches
all the fires and when she finishes herself and turns to him
they play four hands of Messerschmitt & whist
they told him she was
partly Jewish but he thought that was to test the strength
of aileron extension cord
as mummery's   a max of amory's   own   *Pax*
arpeggiate & stringle   D-ring ripnote nein

III

Café des Westens
Kurfürstendamm

1.

                where we waited for that Bruckner
concert to begin, drinking beer, remembering
especially how the great Wilhelm
Furtwängler conducted the adagio when Father
did it in his study Führer
in his bunker muted cellos in Berlin even better than
Vienna even back when Rupert Brooke sat
writing at our table about Grantchester, the Vicarage,
the clotted cream on ripe
berries, blood
a trifle if there's just enough for tea
just enough tradition that's behind it all when
Isherwood and Auden came out for
the boys working class the best
ass of course and free of bourgeois English scruples
about heavy brass and soaring violins
klezmer music too although by that time Jews
were you know Schoenberg Britten both
wrote songs for cabaret says *humm*
it for me Mr Bowles (Paul, that is, working here
with Copland then) or Sally
named for him in fiction odd as that may sound
but sally forth

2.

to old Vienna. Did you know I wrote an honors thesis
at Ohio State on Isherwood?
Yes and met him once of twice. Flakey don't you know
but helped me out a lot and introduced me
to his more important friends.
More important anyway than he was. Who
was greater, Furtwängler? Or do you think von Karajan?
A Brahms by the latter someone once
described—all the timpani ablaze—as witnessing
a person being kicked to death. And then the Swedes
gave their prize to fuck me bite me Jelinek,
professor of piano. Movie, too. Her student beats
her up; she likes it, Erika,
and she sleeps with her own mum.
Hitler was a Catholic. My Notre Dame students
always choke on that.
Ich bin ein Berliner. Mr Gorbachev tear down
this wall. A British diplomat in code to Whitehall once:
I see Joseph Goebbels at a restaurant every
week or so. What about I rub him out, Chicago?
Don't be silly, mon vieux, we don't do diplomacy like that.
1936 or 37. Is it time for that concert?
Oscar Miłosz—and I don't mean Czesław; when
he won the prize I told them damn you've
got the wrong bloody Miłosz—wrote *La Berlin arrêtée*
dans la nuit: en attendant les clefs, waiting
for the keys. It's a kind of hooded carriage, a Berlin,
huddled masses in the church
herded altogether boys out to where

3.

the chairs are all arranged around the tables
at Café des Westens and got off
the bus poor dumb tourists that we were. It was 1961.
Less than twenty years had passed we'd
visited an uncle
of our pal Hans Morton Todd III he was survivor
of a U-boat crew & few enough of those
his daughter there at dinner with her French lover
all stuffed with Sartre.
Was John Hawkes's Spitzen-on-the-Dein a real place?
1949 that book and J.H. only 23
disciple I suppose of Al Guerard who wrote
the Introduction taught us Conrad, Stanford, 1963–65
New Directions books are published always *for*
and never *by* James Laughlin
sole alumnus of the Ezuversity at Castle Soninlaw, Italia.
Hawkes: *Will you tell me what day it is*
Weiss nicht
Do you know what year it is
Weiss nicht
Do you know where you are
Weiss nicht
We knew that it was Friday, 1961, Berlin,
our well-connected friend Hans Morton Todd III

4.

knew a little German *Kindertotenlieder* for example
little kids & babes firebombed with adults
their mums gone ash and bone and carbon atoms
you'd inhale when you breathed free
as far away as Grantchester. He did indeed the Churchill
darling Brooke write that thing right here
you'd hardly credit it the clotted cream on ripe
berries, blood
but that was still before the First War
a trifle if there's just enough I said already
Horst Wessel Lied
Clio—not the muse of history, my cat—
walks across computer keys and history is purposeful
thought Stalinists and Nazis both
History is not but Clio is stepping down on $ and ! and %
just the way that Anton Bruckner's cat stepped
down on white keys and black
to make it all chromatic just before
she leapt onto the strings themselves thunderous and
avant-garde degenerate entirely in her art.
What Sailor was it like in U-boats what Pierre this
song sings Jean Paul Sartre
we all knew next to nothing in those days

5.

and probably still do. We didn't know
that Lilly Hellman would be played by Jane Fonda
or that "Julia" was really Stephen Spender's lover Muriel
whose *Code Name Mary* broke the cover of a tale
that wasn't true or whether Auden's midrash was sublime
or merely submarine, *halakha* or *aggadah*
forged papers were exchanged
right here and Mary took them to Vienna
just before the Anschluss when she did analysis with Freud
Spender wrote to Isherwood a woman's body's
more than I expected and of real interest more than
any well hung boy's did Hegel say that
History is that which no one wanted History is cats
on keyboards on computer keys mice on
screens and boys hanging from a gibbet or a tree is
doppelgänger doppelzüngigkeit in Eastern sector 1961
the first wire going up and Stasi maybe at the next table
laughing at us as we translate for ourselves
the sign across the street: *Bureau*
of Unusual Events
Nostalgia peaking oddly now for old checkmate
old checkpoint old Charlie
dumping millions in defunct Ostmarks the theatre
of Bertolt Brecht & concrete fact (cement)
our own George Smiley waiting at a bridge for Karla
college girls picking at the loose chunks of wall
to bring home in their backpacks
JFK proclaimed: *I am a doughnut*—a "Berliner"

6.

cunning as the passages in Mahler, Bruckner,
Brahms, the moments when the rival maestros would
outflank each other, speed it up or slow it down
in ways they'd not rehearsed
even to the point the concertmaster gets confused and
skips a phrase the brass and woodwinds
charging some four bars ahead and young Isolde of the
cellos stands and shrieks, pulling off her fishnet stockings
tossing them and then her bra & panties to the
S.S. weepers in the first row
for after all it's Herbie von, after all it's Furtwängler
—the scarecrow and the robot—
while high in the stirrup of his left ear rides
the microfilm that Lord König's agent pressed too hard
into the auditory canal breaching thus
tympanic membrane hammer & the anvil crashing in a
deaf man's forge: *Da stieg en Baum*
all hearing's tallest tree wound up in there but not for
him sings Grantchester the acorn & the oak
and Lebensraum for naiad faun and goat-foot piper
on the mind's table top
a manic Sea Lord mammoth in his mourning at the sacrifice
of young Apollo open cricket shirt & bare feet tickled
into motor cortex by the music
will expand the neural zone and modify the past
oral well before you know what's written
whole cities die in firestorm and
the last horseman of the cavalry at Omdurman
alive in the audience a gaze exchanged
the flash of a dying synapse crash of a falling roof

7.

with advent of magnetic tape the maestros were
denazified—this official, 1947—but only one can see
the future in LPs and studio recording
back in 1939 he lost the thread entirely doing *Meistersinger*
for a gala and the tenor stammers to a halt
the fiddles one by one fall silent down comes the curtain
with the nervous floppings of my sophomore
student offering on classical FM to spin a new CD called
Die, Mister Singer! Sophomores all in 1961
who thought we sat at *that* table when we sit at *this*
the format of the menu dropping from the screen like choices
for an appetizer English titles for a movie on The Wall
regions of the brain areas parietal and medial
that turn on and plunge us in the past happily enough
but startled when we drift from our task
a hand on a cup or stein or instrument or someone's throat
the lobes temporal light up like cities in an MRI
default for Mr. Singer Hellman Isherwood Herr Bruckner
anybody when I think about it clotted cream
was not what he wanted at Café des Westens May 1912
but honey it was not there
but Grantchester in 1961 I was nineteen
I'm sixty five
with no desire for adagio adagio on anybody's birthday
at this table. That one. Above it hover bees

Trigon Two: I–III

SONNET: AUTHOR NOTE, REVISED

John Matthias is Professor Emeritus
At the University of Notre Dame and
Poetry Editor of *Notre Dame Review*.
He has published many books of poetry,

Criticism, and scholarship including
New Selected Poems (2004) and *Kedging* (2007).
He is also a musician and a physicist.
Lecturer in Sonic Arts at the University of Plymouth,

He has worked with many artists
Including Radiohead and Coldcut.
His works and collaborations include

Cortical Songs and *The Fragmented Orchestra*.
He is in fact two persons
And a fiction in this book.

SONNET: TRIGON NOTE, REVISED

No Romans but involving at least two
Players with a right hand and a left.
The right hand may not know what
The left hand is doing

But it doesn't matter any more. An actual
Method of scoring: Players must
Abide triplicity and third harmonic, 120 degrees,
And group signs according to their element.

No Romans, but remains of California 1963–5,
CCCP 1967, Paris 1968,
And London off and on involving two players

Anyway but no Romans. Many changes in
The lineup by the fusion band (1) but
Greek and Roman lutes are herewith disallowed.

———————

(1) Strong band sum is a natural construction from links to dichromatic links. We compute Hoste and Kidwell's dichromatic link invariant of a strong band sum in terms of monochromatic invariants of the data (original link, band). It turns out that the two-variable Conway polynomial of a strong fusion only depends on the monochromatic Conway polynomial of the original link. In particular, it does not depend on the band. Cochran's series of concordance invariants is discussed in this framework.

Partially supported by NATO via DAAD

(Google search: "I'm Feeling Lucky")

I

ROADEX REFLEX

1.

a fluting   D   afloating A   anhip-
pocampus reloops the timbres so you'd recognize it either/or
a violin at junction that's parietal
temporal occipital   you'd recognize a voice   brother/or
sister can you spare a dime for anything millennial
in real time or wrought through neural networks
ecstasy?   readout   a renown
whose red rover sent the wrighter over   Regent for oneself
and pitch as pitch can   rode a motorbike those days
a green Rabbit in from Mountain View
the place I lived two years and had myself checked out
for radiation now and then fearing as I did
proximity to linear accelerator that was always firing something
at me in my slum apartment at the end of that contraption's
rifle barrel
              D driving & already doubtless weary of my
discourse my anecdotes let's just look at seals
just look at all these rocks this sea
and on the laptop A dear A I hardly dare and after
forty years you'll hardly care (a song *tra la* for amusiac agraphic
palilaliacs perhaps) but looking for
the William Burroughs site up popped your married name
and you in fact professor now of all things
Computer Science
all weirdly wired like those Stanford undergrads long after us
who took the world in their hands and changed it
in a way no poet ever did. We'd have sneered at the advert
in the right margin here where half naked girls
whisper in the ear of Nerd we love it when you talk high tech you
loved it when I talked about my story novel poem play
the book I'd surely write one day had
written and would read to you aloud in bed I didn't
need to write I knew it all
by heart I'd sing it to you like a bloody bard

a bird a bad bad bad   *delete delete*   arousal and reward
lights up the ventral striatum and the amygdala
meter says I love you to a reptile brain   & saw the Watts riot smoke
that drifted all the way into Big Sur our destination
then & now with Jeffers Miller Kerouac for company our books
Esalen baths and Tantric sex you can't really

2.

get there on a bike   the Beat prototype was R.L. Stevenson
I'd say who chased his married Hoosier girl
by ship and train and wagon then on horseback then on foot
from Edinburgh all the way to Monterey
a one-street seasand town where laptop was for
courting sites were places where you'd stand and gaze like
stout Balboa even think about a homestead build
a cliffhung cottage just a little north from where
the Pico Blanco sun at equinox had warmed the bones of
friendly enemies the tribes of men who
settled their disputes by tossing stones like Romans
playing trigon tossed them in a way that every miss was counted hit
until the mission gathered them inside and gave them
measles and diphtheria   TB made RLS an hemorrhagic
scarecrow but he set out up the Carmel valley anyway with
horse and trap *the sound of breakers follows you*
high up into the inland canyons glade thicket grove surround
you follow winding sandy tracks to nowhere
quail arise a multitude a wind among the trees unending
distant rumble of the sea
                        poor RLS we thought, poor
Kerouac dear A   that day we ditched
my bike and took from Gus Mozart's lot (a real name he
even gets a sentence in Hugh Kenner) spiffy new and wholly
adequate Volkswagen bug across from Palo Alto
through the hills to Half Moon Bay and down the coast to
hot springs and Nepenthe where our friends did their drugs and
fucked each other black and blue   poor Jack before
he wrote his last good book a passenger a-rocking in his chair
beside Lew Welch the driver front seat cut away
on right he rocked like Kennedy two years before his death
and talked to Philip Whalen lying on a mattress 1961
it would have been   *delete*

breakman and recaper of old tires didn't go along to
Bixby Canyon didn't like his portrait in his
friend's commemoration of their wild rides together
D and I hear on the radio that Jack's again the news they've
printed after fifty years and more

3.

that scroll   scrawling it by hand all in a rush or
typing for the pleasure of the touch itself—
we've stopped along the coast near Monterey dear A
and look up at the hills above the Carmel Mission RLS looked
down from when he drew Point Sur as if it were
an island *B Minor Mass* we thought could skip the *Dies Irae*
when we heard it in that setting though we met in old San Francisco
gas-lit hallway between Beatles songs and I was still
a music snob so nothing but the Bachs and Britten
were for me and Mozart, Gus—
D points out that Jack has also landed in the US Pleiades the
Lib of Am how pleased he'd be a serious
tragic man who ran with an odd crowd & warrants our respect
our friend V.I. (named for Lenin) rode a real cycle
and I followed on my Rabbit just like Sal ran after Dean & Jack ran
after Neal with his notebook open jotting down the drivel
and the blather for his book—our friend V.I. who died when none
of us were looking, 1993
                              the first poem I wrote that I have
saved & printed many times in over thirty years
was *your* memory not mine I never really swam out naked in
a quarry and at midnight—only wanted to have done it once
you told me how it felt—*the water's mouth and hands that imitated
someone's touch*   it was the title of my book
as well and now in Italian translator Gabriele tells me it
will be *Nuotando a mezzanotte* which is just fine
everything he's done sounds to me like Verdi or Puccini
arias even if you only ask *Dovrebbe, se il telefono suonasse,
rispondere? E se dovessero bussare alla porta?* The question's
always *Who is there?* The answer always *I am*

      late night in Mountain View I heard a
tapping at my window you had come to—
why *had* you come I was never sure it seemed on some compulsion

and you stood at my door you didn't speak I said
What is it and *what is it*   last night we stayed at some
impossible motel on El Camino dirty cheap the only
thing that we could find but when I opened up the door I said
to D my god they've made a shrine of it preserved it
just the way it was in 1963 my room!
a bed a desk an old gas heater on the wall a loo
those old austerities of poverty *E se dovessero busare alla porta?*
Leaking rusty shower's mouth and hands that imitated
someone's touch and D says

4.

What?   What is it   they were filming 1934
along Point Lobos *that* is what   the very tale
he told that hibernated in the map he'd drawn when looking
down on whaler's knoll and noting through
the seasons monkey flowers sun cups seaside thrift
and barking seal pups   the sound techs in early talky
asking Wallace Berry please to speak up now & Barrymore to stand
upwind and wave at *Hispaniola* anchored in the cove
from which the crew waves back as camera pans across the pines
out topping other vegetation & above the pines
rock outcroppings tallest of them sheer on every side
and flat across the top as if a pedestal for RLS
in 1881 entirely ill-advised to start that trek up out of
Carmel Valley dazed & lost and we were ill-advised
to go out with the abalone diver 1963 in high swells just because
the sky was blue and the horizon clear—*look!*
the sea's a quarter inch below the point where it will
swamp the stern and no one even on the shore
to see but him and that was eighty years ago back then and now
another forty—*Long John* a code word of the KGBs
who'd read their *Treasure Island*
though we didn't know it then when Moscow Central
sent their men to study ESP at Esalen
UFOs as well they argued with the Hollywood producer
that the aliens were not the same as Christian angels
Leary was an alien for sure and if you stayed for long you
learned the angles earned your own way
weird that we were forced to stop our conversation once
some druggie shouting *you can't talk about that, man*
that happened in the group it's privileged, man
though neither you nor I nor Bob had ever been at Esalen
bathing naked in the bubbling mellow springs nor
in a group & therefore were not bound by Moscow rules—
Thrill me somehow you had said pretend that I'm

your Tantric sister or a spy I said I haven't *got* a sister and
the spies have all become the heads of state
computer techies unacknowledged legislators do you
see that boat says D it's in a deep trough and real danger
Hispaniola first imagined breaking through a fog
and no one on the island but the man who told Jim Hawkins

5.

I'm marooned   well not exactly A but what's a life
in Bettendorf Columbus or South Bend if not
marooned I've been a landlocked Indiana resident for forty years
while you departed Iowa for good and
settled up the coast while here they crossed the bridge on Highway 1
over Bixby Canyon where we'll be in half an hour
poor Jack sleeping on the cliff-face calling his hallucinations
Flying Horses of Mien Mo—no one would pick up
the seedy sorry man who tried to hitch a ride even though
they might have all been reading his last book he
couldn't stomach—later 60s—all the hip young things he'd call into
existence he was patriotic damn it and would
kick their ass—
                   I don't know but I was only Regent then
and now a roving laptop onlie true begetter Apple
did not need a flying horse or sail to catch the wind but just
a small garage in Palo Alto once we'd left
I wrote about the Hedy origins of spread-spectrum template 1941
in *ballet mécanique* John Pierce himself of Bell Labs & Telstar
ending up at 80 in the 90's SU well after CCRMA's acoustical
good-karma-avant-garde fussed sufficiently with sine wave frequencies
to fix parameters and modulate their way to Yamaha
before the Google twins Brin & Page emerged from that same
matrix moving into Mountain View no longer
scorched irradiated earth for poet's digs or Orphan Annie slum
but Mien Mo of ever-sleepless eye scanning the entire world
once we're underneath somebody's Wi-Fi umbrella
we can type in JM Music we can bring Matthias in from Plymouth
firing neurons in his *Cortical Songs* which may be how
we'll do it in the future when the green Rabbit that we ride is something
bioengineered by Eduardo Kac a transgenic poetry
or xenographic transplant scriptogenesis with real ears instead
of merely handle bars
over which I flew when some nitwit on a dark and stormy night

pulled out in front of me and after that the next thing
I remembered was V.I. beside me in the ICU holding my I.V. and saying
do you want me to phone A? They don't know how badly
you are hurt
      but it was over then you didn't dress my wounds
didn't knock again against my window pane or door
only ditzy movie stars are married just one year and not the
likes of us but plenty of them at Nepenthe
looking at the view between the takes of *Comus*: *Not that*

6.

Nepenthes which the wife of Thone
in Egypt gave to Jove-born Helena is of such power to stir up
joy such as this   we saw that film eventually
with Rock Hudson John Milton
Glen Ford and Ms MacLaine (Shirley) who would tell all
in her memoir   better than the RLS of 1934
of course technology by then had been improved and I'm a fit
audience though few
                             even Miller thought he saw the UFOs
attests to that in *Big Sur . . . the Oranges of Bosch*
you can bring in JM now Semblable and your namesake
doppelgänger on the new connect says D we're close enough
to mesh network hotspot IEEE 802.11 UC
Santa Cruz and Monterey—*so sing*
spiking neurons synchronizing patterns fed as MIDI data manifest
as light all plasticity synoptic voltage beyond threshold
some potentiated some depleted in the x-axis y-axis unpredictable
but never random it's a music that results from these events
that trigger an array of oscillators signal to the Ten Tors Orchestra
and JM improvising violinist check it out at songscortical.brain
or Plymouthmusicwhatthefuck.mind
it's real enough says D although of course it isn't you
Henry Miller saw *a blue-green hue pervading distant hills*
as from an old Flemish or Italian master
fall of light in bent rays that gleamed and sparkled in a way
that one couldn't tell at first when turning toward the sea if any
thing approached—the abalone boat whose pilot risked
our lives by going out at all or *Hispaniola*
once no more than synchronizing patterns of the spiking
neurons in a sick man's daze—*Sing*
Perishing Republic once was in anthologies you read
at school Jeffers' flinty chiseled stare right there on *Time's* cover 1932
but no it's *Shine! Perishing Republic*
while America thickens to an Empire there's always

consolation in the insolent silence of the stone
the convicts building Bixby Canyon Bridge four years before
and UFO perhaps the USN Dirigible in fog the *Macon*
biwing tenders buzzing round it
bees almost extinct already here and elsewhere
down below 1000 feet and upside down the chassis
of a car beneath the bridge and A you said
why don't we pick that seedy sorry hitcher up and D says

7.

don't   you think they'd pitch him through at
eight-oh-two-eleven   timbre
of a movie babe in white nightgown all sustained appoggiatura in
a spotlight falling from the clef   frequency
quite different from a widow in the forest with a single candle
in her window or a man with a railway lantern riding
like a surfer on a wave—
piggybacking sans encryption by default the OS X picks up
whatever network's strongest on the little
bridge the *sul ponticello*   A=440 Hz and D's a little sharp
but *are you there* and *are you there*
to catch a wave or hitch a ride on text or song and
god only knows and god only knows what we did with all
the multiplying integers of one another all
the overtones of things in underbrush at six percent for
each step we took & your treading doubled
inland twelfth root of two god only knows the *Ohrwurm*
playback of the roadex brings up with the ear worm reflex
warnings from a time I'd lost to old models
Hispaniola laid a couple points
nearer to the wind an anchorage in sight
the early morning grays all yellows now and greens of sand
and trees   hitcher was the abalone diver
and we never should have taken up his invitation driven down
the old dirt wagon path to where he had his boat
I clung to the backstay once we were a quarter mile out & she was
rolling scuppers rudder hanging to and fro get hold of it
get hold of *yourself* you said the more afraid you are the less
our chance of making it   Watts towers rising in LA
through all the smoke of urban riot like a dream of Gaudí steeples
in a poet's Barcelona Robert Duncan writing
of them *art dedicated to itself*—   *delete*

or why not *send* where everything below is sand
and rock and sea a message from the edge of things the edge of

a continent and slipping memory nepenthe's pharmakon
a laudanum to quaff that's born in digitals and not
a crystal glass   we're now the other side of Bixby Canyon
and the signal's breaking up   the song's
unsinging so,   so long

II

Aruski Rehab

1.

   . . . alum from Esalen sat through safe-house
afternoons in Spaso Place unbugging lamps and fixtures
in her mind as the ambassador himself
directed work on redwood hot tub where diplomacy could be
less formal and in fact stark naked
odd to think all this was under Reagan though we might
remember Nancy had her own psychics
in the days John Denver sang *Let us Begin* and Russian healers
walked by moonlight widdershins around
the long and short of *Wo Es War* a great distance from the days
in London when Diana had been positively vetted
and been turned down for service in The Firm because she
lived at sister Lady Kennet's place and had been seen
with people like myself at Covent Garden
shouting *Bravo! Bravo!* at the end of *Onegin*
and *The Queen of Spades, The Gambler* and *The Nose*
I was a fan of Russian opera then & D was
a language student of the former secretary of the
British CP in Hull whose standing joke was that
she had "connections"—meaning that she met a lot of
Labor Party types among the toffs and tipplers just by virtue
of her fashionable address on Bayswater Rd.
everybody had a file at MI5 in those days even Harold Wilson
if you know that name myself I lived in Islington
with Igor who was busted for inciting riots on Trafalgar Square
and photographed at Heathrow handing over papers to
the agents from Hanoi it was a heady time that first trip to
CCCP disguised as a musico-literary scholar when I
hitched a ride on Charlie Newman's manuscript (Ilyushin)
Child's History (Swallow Press, 1969) it would record
what he was doing there but leave me out entirely which was
what I asked—

  I thought I might obtain an interview with
Shostakovich Charlie saying why not try for Guy Burgess

that would be a real coup I'll give you his address
you like to play at spies and this would be the real thing of
course so *Wo Es War Soll Ich Werden* don't you
think? I thought it odd that D had been recruited by the
Russian Orthodox babushkas rather than the MI5
by charismatic Bishop Anthony as chorister at Enismore Gardens
all presided over by the family of Aliosha Behrs

2.

grandson of Sonia Tolstoy's brother.
                                        The sign would be an
overcoat hanging on a park bench beside the
Neva with a nose wrapped in pages from Akhmatova's
Poem Without a Hero in the pocket
Igor was to stay in Islington waiting for the word from me
since he couldn't manage after all to make the trip
busy as he was as wine steward in the house of
Doctor Wisdom (actually a person, you can look him up)
which we rented as a *Home Without a Zero*
it befuddles to this day real estate agents and philosophers
globalized economists and simple thieves
who may have been invited to the same conference
*Music and Your Memory: A.R. Luria and students to
administer the Luria-Nebraska Neuropsychological exam
comparing a placebo group to brain-computer interface
results from dead composers cyrosuspended in
the crystal of their songs*
                        so if you wished to send
a trace through time alone you needed all
the precious five—a way to touch the sound and sound
the depth of seeing hear the color shaping as an image while you
sniffed the brandy of the damned delighted in the flavor of
the yellow flower blooming from a chord   Charlie feared at once
that he was being watched   his watermarked stationery
headed *Young Americans Abroad for Harmony*
had been suspected from the first as alluding to a fiction
where in fact his character a black Maoist wanted as
a dissonant in North Carolina had been sent to steal a cello
once played by Rostropovich for a gangster patron of *Triquarterly*
who wanted it to bribe the LSO first chair to play the last choir
of *Red Dawn* throughout the middle movement of the Old
Commission thus forcing Solti to throw up his arms and shout
that's what comes of only two rehearsals, union members!

leading Charlie in his turn to write of adepts and colleagues
that they had *grown up in a country in which*
every street corner sported aide-mémoire in shape of
new church looking like a filling station or a bank
and now it should be elementary and essential for them all to
go hear instead the music of an Orthodox Cathedral all
graffitied & surrounded by a high iron fence with razor wire
under which the blind peasant women crawled to kiss
the feet of a torn and rusted icon

3.

    although back in London we could see clearly
in the photographs at Enismore Gardens that
an airbrushed version of both that and the other scenes was
to be preferred. All the old babushkas who were often
princess this or princess that objected to our visits to the embassy
where we liked the classic films and vodka after—*Nevsky*
with a re-synched Prokofiev and bootleg versions of the anecdote
about how everything derived from just one sound
the screeching of a train roaring through the station at Smolensk
on which a mnemonist examined by the Luria disciple
mapped the synesthetic pathways through a country village where
he'd placed every note as a word like *umbrella cat gazebo
samovar toysoldier effigy* beside a fence or on a porch or
underneath an apple tree while he sped on by trying to forget his fear
of Schumann's A the end of hallucinations starting with
edenic sounds becoming louder and demonic their sublimity
reduced at death to just one note that burned in his syphilitic brain
and loud and *laude* carried him like Giovanni
down
    we asked Igor once we'd prehabilitated
if he'd got our message he said *no* about *abort*
the short response to *Rimsky* listed still as *Korsakov*
five bottles of the best wine simply vanished down the drain or
were they poured in libation onto Marx's grave the brainbook
reminds us that the eye takes in a word as a word
the corresponding birdbook is organized by region bird by bird
no copyediting Cyrillic ornithologist need intervene
unless a rook or nightingale passing through the scene distract
attention from the battle on the ice
defects of memory are problems of perception in aruski rehab
skripka is not *skrepka* violin is
not to be confused with paperclip photoreceptors
capturing the light as *two dfifenert iamegs on lfet dan rihgt rteniae
dpeenindg no the smeihpor dcoednig eclertctiy as*

ees or feel or haer korPvoeiv coabllortaed ni a yaw on
cposomer eevr dah bferoe with a dricetor children making
toy suits of armor out of paperclips and Eisenstein painting all the
trees with white and salting every extra just so you keep
the first and last letter plucking pizzicato
on mnemonic violin—
                        skripka is skripka
and so we had eventually a house in London
and a flat in Moscow and our six friends in Leningrad with whom we
always stayed in Petersburg close enough

4.

to be a fair distance on   Or for that matter
some distance off.   The handles on the water taps
to our surprise didn't say *hot* or *cold* in any language we could read
but *bought* and *sold* in several   in her bath
Tatiana raised a fetching leg high above the suds
billowing in that same tub where after she had gone we would
wash the dishes and the silver from the conference feast.
Witzelsucht the tenor said you've got the wisecrack disease
coming on you with Tourettic consequence.
Charlie had revealed in his *History* of 1968 that our first trip
had ended for him not at the conference where his
paper on Scriabin's synesthesia had been picked to pieces by
the delegates from China but inside the ZIV limousine
from which a child with Williams Syndrome beckoned to him
singing *Tolstoy and Lenin in the end were both*
convinced they had to wring the neck of music fifty rubles for
your Dacron socks—
                    pitched at 440 cycles every second and
an amplitude of 60 decibels you see
the credits on the screen the rolling titles pitched at
523 cycles amplitude of 90 decibels the view from Pereyaslavl
and the frozen lake pitched at 622 cycles amplitude of 120 decibels
a flash of lightening and the Teuton cavalry advancing
like a Panzer unit on the ice 880 cycles amplitude of 180 decibels
the ice breaks and Comrade Stalin with a perforation of
your eardrums and a sunblast on your retinas transmutes the cycle
into cyclotron   amplitude to grim necessity
black & white to work & war the minor keys to miners' fees
and Tatiana's exit to a steppe flower swallowed by
a Tuvan watching movies in the Urals at the moment you write down
the name they wanted and the pseudonym as well.
Old stories certainly but this was the second trip when I was sent
back from lecturing on *Ballet mécanique* in NYC
aboard the *Lermontov* presumably to disembark with D at

Thames side dock electronic thumb as I recall it now
in *Wikipedia* D's *Britannica Eleven* swallowed there where now
you find the peasants stripping Diderot from
Catherine the Great—

                                            pheasant for the dinner Lady K
prepared while D was hiding in a priest hole thinking
Lord Protector I was working on the hydrodynamics for my *Crossing*
asking what makes waves?
as if one thought that rehabilitated phonemes for the ball were photons
and we ought to make our own

5.

separate peace with history. But *what? makes? waves?* components
of resistance? poets must as ships do dear encounter
counter count on it: who waves at signals lovingly what wives
await returning man he shanty sings of sea-born signs
Potemkin Homer Mayakovsky Virgil Quote: *Then first the river
hollowed alders felt . . .*
                            and by that means I'd gone
again to Leningrad. The text of *Crossing* asked for
a conclusion and I wrote myself into a narrative I didn't follow
past the ghostly Kelmscott oarsmen estuary chains
Gordon fortifications stone outcroppings along the Hundred of Hoo
and through a Dickensian fog all the way to Bayswater Rd.
By then I'd said goodbye to D and still on the *Lermontov* was
navigating through the Stockholm archipelago and
Gulf of Finland to fulfill an obligation to the six I'd left in Petersburg
who went out to the theatre where it was Lermontov . . .

  his *Masquerade* . . .   Shostakovich
might have made an opera of it if they
hadn't executed Meyerhold but that comes
later on   Tonight it's Meyerhold's production it is no
ordinary evening in October   Everybody's there   everybody who
is anybody's there but Anna Andreyevna only managed
tickets for rehearsal isn't anybody who is anyone
just yet   when she leaves a dress shop in the afternoon it all begins
it all begins like theatre like *Masquerade* like Lermontov
it all begins like Meyerhold perhaps those mummers
mime it all perhaps the bodies lying in the street are only doused
with buckets of red paint   the painters all come too the painters
and the dancers and the violinists mime   All the dead men
get back up to much applause all the dead men lie there in
the streets and either way Anna Andreyevna tastes her
Tartar blood and speaks she makes a music of this Meyerhold
this masquerade   the lovesick Gumilyov tells her he

is dead a suicide Gumilyov is not dead he only mimes he's shot
of course but that comes later on   it's Knyazev who's
killed himself for love   Who will die for Vladimir Ulyanov?
Everyone who goes to *Masquerade* she'll write it down
they write down everything you say the ones who ask you where
you live who ask your name who ask you why you're
playing in this masquerade while Petersburg is burning down it is
revised with major cuts provided by the censors
Petersburg by Boris Nikolayevich Bugayev the symbolist Bely
where Nikolai Ableukhov stands

6.

before his mirror as a domino in an assassin's mask
his hand upon a bust of Kant—
who can't tell you what the mummers in the poem by
Anna Andreyevna mimed from another age
on the Fontanka it was privileged where she conjured up a
guest from the future bringing doom instead
of flowers where she wrote upon the writings of the dead
there's Mandelstam *there's* Meyerhold *there's* Blok
where the Engineer of Souls was whispering *we'll melt your
triple-bottomed black
libretto down into a hymn of state and gift you with a row of dots
out of Onegin*—
                          nonetheless, Leonid Brezhnev's psychic
healer who was called Dzhuna Davitashvili
really did meet with Apollo astronauts two decades after
I'd gone back and Luria who wrote his book in 1968 but studied S
his patient from the 20s on fascinated Eisenstein so much
because he showed him just the way that S
remembered everything by placing objects of perception
thought imagination on an infinitely winding road down which
enlarged Hippocampus strolled asking in the
key of B *what's the difference between Masha Marusya
and Mariya* an interrogation Eisenstein adapted interviewing
new projectionists S knew that *Masha* was a tall thin babe
with pointy tits *Marusya* was a plumpkin but she had a pretty smile
and *Mariya* was an icon Charlie wrote about it in his *History*—
"graffitied church surrounded by a high iron fence
with razor wire under which the blind peasant women crawled" etc—
I had it in italics in part two but this time it's in quotes
Poor Charlie died last year   But Igor's writing up a memoir that
he'll call *The House of Professor Wisdom* and he asks me
in an email as I'm writing this if I can tell him anything I think
he should omit from such a rehabilitation—grounds of
personal embarrassment or what's it called

Official Secrets Act?   D is in the kitchen and I can't clearly hear
what she says—
                          don't rehash an old Rus rehearsal if it
wasn't habitable then it's not habilitated now
it may have been
habitué of all my past performances she'd read me Pushkin
played mazurkas on her sister's harpsichord
and after all my journeys to the *Wo Es War* of things she'd welcome
me with Brussels sprouts

7.

and mangelwurzels—beetroot for cattle if you have to play it
in the key of C
                        CCP because that lunch was for the founders
of Choleric Conference on Contemporary Poetry
as it became in the days of Gorbachev and Yeltsin when the visas
came through easily enough and old dissidents were disregarded by
the avant-garde while Esalen packed the galleries to argue for poetics
of a Tantric Resurgence and an end to ordinary history
with citizen diplomacy and ESP for all—
My own job by then was to cultivate nostalgia for the good old days by
meeting periodically with (soon to be known as agent) Blunt
who had a fondness for Diana's cooking   Igor was a little slow
to place the friend who came along with B asking if he'd
met the Director at the Courtauld or shared an interest in Poussin
he said in fact the two had met inside the public
loo at Tottenham Court Rd wasn't it a pity about Perestroika

The good old days   did I really love the Ruskies and their
Revolution   Fellow Travelers   Trotskyites
the way I thought when I began letting people know
in Indiana and Ohio how I'd been a communist beginning at
the age of twelve and then became a dissident
MI5 and George Smiley leading Karla to the wall and reading
late at night *Zhivago* at the same time listening to the Shostakovich 5th
you wouldn't like it any more than I if someone pulled your
fingernails out with rusty pliers did you know the
human nose keeps growing during one's entire life a scientific fact
the scent of eidetic memory will conjure even when you
concentrate on melody the Nevsky Prospekt well before the KGB
the good old days before Sir Anthony (the traitor Blunt)
was banned from banquets at the Palace and began to eat
with us the good old days well before
the good old days when grandfather still was young
and read the first Englishing of *Kreutzer Sonata* but begat

my father and his siblings anyway   though not with his nose
which started walking through the streets of Van Wert, Ohio
thinking it was harbinger of me and Charlie Igor D and Lady K
years before I went to Russia or to Britain either one
years and years before I was even born
good times were had by all it wore a long mustache and smelled
the pancakes and the rumors from abroad
have a good breakfast and a show trial for all there will be
in the passage masquerade &
nothing funny about that except the laughs

III

Chez Harvey Goldberg

1.

        & I suppose you could call it business & pleasure
the pleasure part of it a honeymoon of sorts
before the wedding six months away and staying with
my old teacher Harvey Goldberg or at least
at the same hotel he lived in while in Paris working on the life
of Jean Jaurès   HG himself I'd call a great
orator like J—you should have heard him on those big years
1789   1848   1870—he'd take off his glasses
and the *music of revolution* nothing else can say what it was like
flooded into mid-America   I hoped he'd approve
of D given all his strictures on "the girlfriends of poets" as he'd
say derisively and I could tell in an instant that he'd
been completely smitten   Funny how charisma really is
enough because he was a strange looking man
and not a person you would think could have both girls & boys
rolling in his sheets   Sartre was just the same
although he wasn't interested in boys and Harvey wasn't
wall-eyed
           Chez Harvey Goldberg   with some glee he
passed the letter old Captain Adams D's father wrote to
the address of that hotel thinking it a private home
Harvey said to D ah! you're smart as Simone de Beauvoir & twice as
beautiful here's a letter must be from a parent
I believe . . . Generations! And we had such a sense of our own
everybody does I suppose everybody's is the best
of times the worst of times and all of that but D and I as well as
on this kind of honeymoon had work to do
and Harvey said I feared she'd be a blue-stocking
or a femme fatale
                   Jean Jaurès feared worse but fared well
before the 1898 election when on May 8th cyclists from
the villages brought news of his defeat by the new right alliance
of Solages who spooked the constituents with charges J was
anticlerical and Dreyfusard and agent of Freemasonry to boot

though J had trudged through rain and mud to speak in barns & stables
standing up on barrels haystacks wagons crying Common cause
my brothers with the miners or Carmaux
an old peasant shouted back But you're the one who wants to
tear down churches J replied
and what do you think I'd do with all those stones
pile them in 1968 perhaps beside some burned out cars along
the Boulevard Saint-Germain with toppled

2.

plane trees and the uncollected garbage of another May
the 24th imagination or a 6th sense
trying to take power   HG would take us to see Sartre
eventually but we were tourists for a while in spite
of tear gas down around the Sorbonne   did you know that
J-PS kept yo yos in his pocket and was good at tricks
like spinning them or doing left hand yo out horizontally while
right hand yo went up and down? he'd wait in line outside
the cinema for yet another showing of the John Ford *Stagecoach*
both yos whizzing just a craze and just a phase in Paris
for a while but not allowed in Stalag XII-D where he was sent
in 1941 the year come to think of it that I was born
and almost by reflex the association with that yo & muscle memory
connect while still typing here and bring in the *belle époque*
of Fauré and Franck the cellist Ma from iTunes
intimations of or maybe even the exact phrase in one of these
sonatas that for stunned Marcel in time for time
regained brought back a life entire although god knows
it's not the best marching music
for the days of May   D said what would Maigret do
in such a situation I said *what* situation she said
well he often found the bodies in hotels
and in a way they were his thing living often in a place
like this La Louisiane at 60 rue de Seine founded 1823 by
old *grognard* of Bonaparte so upset by homelessness
among old comrades that he built them this place as
a boarding house & now our chez HG where people lived from
time to time like Bardot and Charlie Parker Miles Davis
Jim Morrison and Bertrand Tavernier who would in 1986
make that film *Round Midnight* all about Bud Powell who
lived here too and set it partly in a room
right down the hall—
          Maigret in *Pietre-le-Letton*
asks to have a place set for himself right beside
his quarry in the hotel dining room eats his dinner drinks his coffee

then looks up and says   I think your false mustache
is falling off   his maker Simenon using a vocab of just 2000 words
to write some 200 books one about a man in one room without arms
who's cuckolded by someone in another without legs
one about two bodies stuffed in lockers in the Hotel Majestic
he liked *fatalement balbutier hallucinant* and *il s'est mis à boire*
Harvey liked a rhythm sometimes biblical & sometimes
just a little bit like Ezra Pound

3.

at 84 years old he said the hero of Verdun is in good shape
and married to a girl of twenty-one   He's got just
two passions left   the infantry and sex
although suffice to say he's rather ga-ga as a leader not quite
with it really not quite there   he goes to sleep
in meetings about marshalling the tanks and then wakes up
to talk about how well the use of homing pigeons
works when all other forms of contact with the high command
have been cut off from Fauré's *belle époque*
which morphs easily ("Description of Pétain") into
Harvey's archived lectures just as well from La Louisiane
as here they've got a Wi-Fi now and group of Linux
software nerds in room 39 Charles Olson mystified the typing on his
silly Royal in *Projective Verse* but we can play a keyboard
now as if it were an organ try the
Goldberg variations   HG Center Madison Wisconsin
http://history.wisc.edu/goldberg/goldberg.htm
after *belle époque* and your Fauré—
                                        D and I of course
had in mind a recess now and then from history
and being tourists both with afternoons in bed and two
electric fans blowing on us it was hot that May
and laughing found in fact that we agreed with La Beauvoir
who moved to room 68 in 1943 and said I'd never
lived somewhere I'd happily have stayed the rest of my
entire life (J-P S in #10) while Simenon had boasted
that he slept with 1500 women just the one Miss A was quite
enough for me my femme fatale blue stocking
of the night in afternoon   but up we'd get at 5:00 for
drinks and dinner then along the little streets
au coeur du Saint-Germain-des-Prés to see the burnings-out
and barricades and hear the speeches music boasting
Sorbonne students who directed traffic proud
of their new occupations now the gendarmes had been driven out

Charlie sees it clearly in his *Child's History* how French
police all use their clubs like swords and not like baseball bats
a subtle thing they think they're musketeers or Roman
legionaries in their capes *touché touché*
they'll get you in the groin they'll get you in the eye or
just below the heart they dance and poke they
dance and poke I'd not seen Charlie since my trip to Russia
he said Well Imagine Meeting You and so forth
there was not a single cop that night on our side of the river

4.

girls dancing with bare breasts and boys kindling fires
on which to cook a meal though the best
restaurants made a point of staying open half the night
where Jean Jaurès had walked the streets
before his testimony in the Zola trial reciting passages
of perfect alexandrines to his friend Anatole France
as preparation for his outcry in the court that
anti-Semites anti-Dreyfusards anti-Republicans among
the military prosecuted him who in *Germinal*
announced the drive of an impoverished proletariat rising
from the depths of suffering ascending
toward the sun Charlie saying that tomorrow
J-PS would talk to them but that we ought not expect
a fireworks display of dialectics for to some extent
he didn't really get it to a very large extent
they didn't get him either trade unionists would only
back the students briefly and de Gaulle would
rehabilitate the fascist generals from Algiers to put it down
and here I flip an email off to Michael A in Austin
asking When you published Charlie's book who did
the work on crafting every page so well
as to accommodate the marginalia that amplifies
or undercuts his argument or sometimes only makes you laugh
his note e.g. that even now I fail to recognize
passing through its discourse in the hall?—Lawrence Levey
il l'a fait says M just as he did your own two books
remember that it's all contra Icarus in honor of apprentice
M. Talos him of the potter's wheel and saw
who was murdered for his simple competence a value
Charlie honored till he died—
                              & Talos it is it isn't
Telos Charlie said I know your friend
Goldberg well enough myself to put you in my book as
staying at a small hotel and not a private home

although as was the case in Leningrad and Moscow I am
nowhere to be seen
even though I sawed the planks and turned the wheel
with all the energy that I could summon up
Jaurès pleading under red flags for peace in 1913 Sartre
before the students Grande Amphithéâtre
on 20 May of 68 greeted by a chant *Nous ne voulons pas
des personalités* he's sick and old and patient
almost blind they call him Jean-Paul
and no one ever called him that he was just Sartre

5.

his doctors tell him that his hypertension is so bad
a confrontation with a crowd (a mob?) might kill him
all of this tomorrow Charlie says
the waiter takes my plate away the portly gentleman
beside me says your false mustache
is falling off—
                      but chez Harvey Goldberg that's ok
as is *Ma femme à la taille de loutre entre les dents du tigre*
ma femme à la bouche de cocarde et de bouquet
d'étoiles de dernière grandeur
and D says with a waist of an otter in a tiger's jaws?
with the mouth of cockade and clustering maximal stars?
Bien sûr I say and white teeth like spoors of mice
on white earth although Mme Breton was not an English girl at
chez Harvey Goldberg *Ma femme aux hanches de lustre*
et de pennes de flàche becomes graffiti on the
walls of air and our small hotel our own arrondissement
though all of this is after dinner in the night
surrounded by the bonfires and the flashlights signaling
through smoke and low-drifting tear gas this is
the way to the liberated Odéon where
on ne parle pas avec des gens qui n'existent pas and so
of course the false mustache must go

I wonder what HG would make of ViaFrance.com and
tourism portals on the Net and start-up companies and Kudzu
in his old room and New Econ tenants and the board
meetings in the mezzanine where we'd meet for morning coffee
looking right across the street at butcher shop and
cheese shop and fish arriving fresh from the morning's catch
with Gallimard the great publisher square in the middle now
of revolution that will make it obsolete books replaced
by what a Cal Tech ViaFrance advisor calls
a better kind of software

                              if you access the HG site from
La Louisane you can hear him
saying   And I saw it coming all of it you know the way I guess
the birds look at bulldozers coming at the trees it was
the post-war war for consumer money & machines to begin with
that would make you laugh like the tiny fridge obtained
by J-P S well no one had a fridge in those days he said he had
a great thing to show me   I said *Ah! C'est formidable*
what else could I say you've got a great refrigerator there but
that was just the first of ten thousand other

6.

gadgets yet to come you plugged in you turned on he also said
you know the people's opium is opium
and of the New Left   when will all of that catch up
with me?—
                we saw them smoking dope and dropping acid
there around their fires
and snorting coke and all the things one did in those days
HG said J-PS stayed fit on Corydrane and Orthodrine
uppers downers inbetweeners all washed down
with red wine or gin while working fifth of scotch at night

his voice was so certain and his certainty a blast
from history about a future which has now
become the past & it will take much longer than he thought
for words to put on flesh and exit Chez HG
on down the Rue de Seine in any way but in a poem
of which the site is maybe now
a spent force the music of a bootleg virtuoso playing at
an rpm of ten beyond the 68 it represents the rasp
of a steel needle in the groove but
nonetheless it sings and off went everyone to revolutions per
the insight of their numbers and you just implant
a chip to regulate your heart for love
and next your brain   and why not your will?   look out!
you'll be some pixels in a program on another's screen
it won't be nice chez quelque chose as they pursue whatever
kind brother rhetoric of Jean Jaurès
who tried to stop a war with strange loops of words
they'll strip it down to Möbius or stripe of
color maybe on a street that otherwise is black and white
but off we go—
                the sight of others marching round
in circles caught us by surprise the
strange loop down Rue Jacob then across the Rue de l'Université

to Gallimard on Rue Sebastian Botain and round
the corner on the Rue du Bac and on to Pont-Royal and
then the Boulevard de Saint-Germain
and there was Charlie pressed against a doorway seeking
with the handle of an umbrella
mischief to make among the Gaullists who were racing
to catch up with Vichy collaborators
racing to catch up with Old Regime aristocrats in powdered wigs
taunted by the crew of Jean-Luc Godard his hand-held camera
looping in the hands of his mistress perched atop

7.

a statue of David drawing in his sketchbook
M-Antoinette playing *La Chinoise*   and old John and
old Diana femme fatale and blue stocking
lost in nostalgia limbic system's hippocampus glowing brightly
chez Cockade and homo erectus wearing
on his head a French horn while quoting Robespierre and
standing on a drum   Charlie said
you missed tomorrow altogether did you spend the day
in bed? I told you he would be there and
he was but didn't really like the crowd and tried to run
a seminar they whisked him in the end to the *Deux Magots*
but what is next that this way comes
bearing on the crest of its wave Ministre d'Etat who once
was the Resistance darling known
to some as Colonel Berger—
                                       700,000 smug bourgeois in suits & ties
all for Referendum: Long live the General
Vive de Gaulle   we're caught up in the wrong parade
and so is history that circles on without Jaurès
without Danton and soon without both J-PS & Uncle Harv
that's what happens if you sleep right through
tomorrow altogether in your curtained room and that's
what happens if you're caught up in the wrong
bloody memory inhabiting the wrong program yesterday's
a typing error in the last oration for the first man there
and yet with any luck today's right poem in spite
of tripping up at trigon check it out at belleépoque.Franck
or com/watch? Myra Hess from *Hess/Hess* all of it appassionata
all in place at v=lyxn2Y4E but out of it in Paris 1968
or the JM doppelganger in from Plymouth
blazing neurons over iTunes clumsy in the touch
is JM poet of these lines Berkeley in 07 part of that same
trip in *Roadex Reflex*: why=zeeEmwhywhytwopioy ployboy
misplaced and ill-informed and looking ill-advised

to be performing in the chez chaise in laptop white-haired ladies
on his left and on his right the wrong palm a prize
for anybody else who missed
tomorrow   maybe even you   we find of a sudden
that it's Sunday afternoon even if it only comes
in books or bites   and loop on out of counting up the laps
on bikes we pedal toward a bandwidth at the border
sun shining brightly through the revolutions per millennium
turning wheels just as if we'd synced our lips
to come in last or like we'd lost at something just in time

Coda

1.

. . . West End London after twenty years and
all the Londoners are young
and I am old. The women in particular—the girls; the birds—
all in this hot weather wearing little, stripped
for speed as they pass me by
hurrying to get beyond a Britain that just barely still exists
Chinese Indians Africans and Arabs
lovely in their different shades of skin and light clothes
veils of Salome or head scarves fallen on the shoulders
pink & yellow saris or the tight & low cut jeans
cinched with a wide leather belt just above the pubic bone
a glitter of the jewelry in navel lip or nose
and elsewhere doubtless out of sight they stride through
the present with their men who now and then
point to something in the air—
        Nelson's there ok and
he is just the same
the only Old Boy I recognize just now around his square
where oddly I have digs in Suffolk Street
behind the gallery in whose basement shelter dugout low
down and lower day after day
Myra Hess played on. I wrote about it in this book.

Lord K is partially amnesiac but knows his way to members'
dining room while we must find a wheelchair for L
he's off   & we get lost in narrow hallways ask yet
other ancients where to go and double back
on doublebackings in a warren where the clerks scurry and
the secretaries scatter where's the members' dining room I don't
know I'm not a member mate and no one
really recognizes Lord K it's been so long since he attended been
so long since Harold Wilson's cabinet met
these men with automatic weapons are security you needn't be
afraid because our papers have been tied around

our necks with silken ribbons when a long time ago the bombers
still were IRA and not the present lot I sat through
a debate about abortion
                              everybody shook his own
member in the gents but you don't want to do it
in the dining room they'll take away your privileges we haven't
seen you for a long time everybody thought
that you were dead
I say the smoked salmon's awfully good & for the main
course I'll have the peasant   rice pudding   stilton cheese   ex-

2.

presso after thanks or maybe port.
                                      About the other John Matthias
I've been curious since he entered *Roadex Reflex*
on the drive along Rt 1 in California to Big Sur. He didn't know
that he was there or that he had a JM doppelgänger
chasing him around the internet and following his work. I can't make
the Rose and Crown in Sandford on the 7th but I know he's
got a dialogue working in his music between gigs he does with
WaxRoom Coldcut Radiohead Etc where no one's brain is
wired to produce an unpredictable but patterned firing of the neurons
only the guitars. But that's for relaxation or some stash.
When I hum a theme deriving from *the spiking neurons synchronizing*
patterns fed as MIDI data manifest as light all plasticity
synoptic voltage beyond threshold some potentiated some depleted
In the x-axis y-axis unpredictable but never random then he knows
that I've arrived to trigger an array of oscillators that can
signal to all members and in real time. On May 10th we're face to face:
the big rotunda of the BBC's Broadcasting House:
du bleicher Geselle! Da steht auch ein Mensch, and Schubert
just writes chords to start it off:

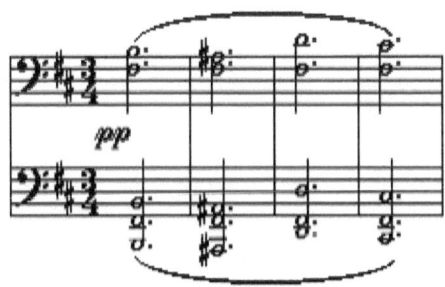

I'm sorry to have chased you all around the world I say
and did you know the half cadence or at any rate the incomplete
progression's in the key of B-minor both creating and traversing what
we hear in *Agnus Dei* of the Mass from June 1828?
I'm sorry also that I've stolen all your stuff but I've been fascinated

and can barely help myself. He's much younger than his double
and reminds me a bit of Joe Francis Doerr. We adjourn across the
street to Songscortical.com where instability of dominant
will surely be increasingly more evident although the four-note
B-A#-D-C# is spiking neurons doubtless now in both our brains while
all the elements of doppelgänger sound in just four bars
and if you soft pedal F# you'll conjure E wringing
hands in Schmerzensgewalt's hermeneutic over pints where he

3.

tells me that the members of his next commission voted on
their independent ley lines for a cortex
made up of neuron units placed throughout the country in
such places as a dairy farm cathedral football stadium primeval
forest ancient castle motorway the Liverpool house
of Paul McCartney underground upon the desk that Churchill
used in Cabinet War Room where *ma femme aux hanches
de lustre et de pennes de flèche* becomes graffiti
on the walls of air
                         all simulated neurons stimulated by
whatever sounds form an instrument comprised
of sound boxes solar powered streaming as a network of
Feonic FI drives and amplifiers 24 channels flowing to a central
space to recombine and broadcast oh just look it up
at www.prsfoundation.co.uk/newmusicaward/index.htm
it's all pretty complicated
though we still look a little like the B-A#-D-C# of things
du bleicher Geselle! Da steht auch ein Mensch
and I've got this text message here from Wilkinson who says
the metaphor's a little strained if we describe the
24 neurons as a human brain   a woodlouse he is sure has
brainpower on a vastly larger scale.

Underground again where I meet D in still another corner
of the poem where I had written of her father walking
through the square and whistling *Pax*
arpeggiated main theme & then *Pay* the trilled figure following
Pax was also known as cockpit section of an aircraft
used for training *Pax* in genetics a transcription factor
of the helix-turn-helix nine member proteins but it wasn't just
training wasn't just practice if you walked whistling through
the sandbagged doors as duty officer reporting *thermite incendiary
hydrants working in this zone* and overheard the PM say
the Deputy has parachuted into Scotland on his own

initiative I simply won't go out tonight to hear that lady play piano in the crypt

                While D deposits in the War Room archive
papers from those days I look at maps and banks
of telephones   the Bell Laboratory Sigsaly Scrambler all
packed in basement rooms at Selfridges with tunnels
through to just one phone just here where PM could whisper
secrets through the relay racks and shifting frequencies to FDR
while D's father pointed at the map which showed the
movement of Icini all along the Icknield Way

4.

great ley line down which strange powers & the old Morgan
Igor let me borrow used to surge—
                              I'd drive from Cambridge
on the A-11 straight toward Thetford
then cut east for Bury and the coast surprised that
my sophisticated lady whom I then associated only with
her eyeshadowed miniskirted urban years had lived so long
a closet blue stocking femme fatale not at chez anything grand
but in Hacheston a tiny village barely on the map
a microdot half an inch from Framlingham I couldn't guess
and would have been incredulous had someone told me
that I'd spend a dozen years myself celebrating roads the dodmen
had aligned on prehistoric equinoxes wells that bent
the dowser's rod the old stones the shingle beach and single
sailors kedging over sandbars or the Nine Men from
somewhere in beyond imploring Wandil's favor as they rowed
the Alde from Orford Ness to Snape Bridge
backs against the morning sun oars against the tide
ings: *Crooked age on three knees creeps the street*
unless you pick a single rose and
leave it in the Aldeburgh churchyard all aflame
on Ben Britten's grave and maybe even if you do
dare to kiss betimes upon the grass or
in the hay: fly Venus and Phlebotomy instructed by the song
a strange verse a strange goddess that Phlebotomy
they'll test your blood for poison even when you conjure up
already health and merriment in June from JM1
to JM2: I'd place a solar powered sound box here the bells
ring it's someone's wedding and although
the rental that we drive isn't Igor's Morgan any more and all
the peddlar's way to Hacheston and Fram is just
a path for drovers with their sheep that rematerialize beyond
the Norman tower you can turn with Feonic tuning
surfaces adjacent into loudspeaking stone click here to let

us know your thoughts you'd never guess the
rigid father on the tomb of Henry Howard was the boy
who broke out windows of the London burgesses
and stepped from prison in the Fleet to legend in the gallery
at Arundel and Thomas Nashe's prose I said
and D says watch your driving stay for heaven's sake
on the right side left side of the road
a shield's quarterings could spell the end of such a man as you
and no one laughed before the scaffold
that he mounted in a January rain of the next year—

5.

who didn't as in Nash carry heraldry of love before
ambition—*militat omnis amans* and a knotted sword—but
bore off into battle on a quarter of his shield
sign of him who'd be an heir apparent poet that he thought
he was—
          or just a single missing gene enough for
Lesch-Nyhan syndrome touched
the tender button 4 awaiting JM2 from BBC his taped program
not yet on but grim assessment of the Lesh-Nyhan
by a doc that's treated those who bite their fingers off who eat
their lips and tongue   if a poem had Lesch-Nyhan it would
eat itself starting with a word or two and then a passage
and if not restrained would aruski rehab roadex reflex chez harvey
goldberg gorge itself on bad-karma avant-garde
and sine wave frequency to fix parameters and modulate beyond
irradiated earth   if some poet had it he would
chew the fingernails the cuticles of writing hand until it bled his wife
would take him to the dentist have his teeth extracted saying
eats everything and is a danger to himself & others
if an old man had the syndrome he would chew his past like cud
praying for robotics to evolve a system where he'd download
himself his mind & soul & be immortal and if JM2's computer
program had it ah but
                    2 on 4 displaces the concerned and patient
doctor's voice it's all Heraldic once again
he promises this tech of artificial cortex made of artificial
neurons will by god rebeam to Britain Britain's song singing self
into existence typing at my task on 15 June 08
I'm interrupted by a phone call saying   *Leila's born*
little girl keep me from my nightmares when I write granddaughter
bring your mother peace   daughter bring your daughter
love   grandfather don't give up your work
when fists clench and palms bleed you suck your lower lip
don't put your tongue between your teeth

don't get too close to other people if a doppelgänger had
the syndrome

JM2 is well into his gig on 4 and JM1 is back on track
trace elements of trigon for an old war drafting back to ball & lute
triplicity and third harmonic fire   water   earth
shadow-play Karaghiosis as the hero & Spiridion the saint in Paris
the pornographer receives a Zero letter in heraldic hand
I fear a war is coming on
the parachutes will flower from the bellies of eviscerated

6.

Icari . . .
            cacophonous and fearful as the lights in air
and tracers flash-lit wing and tail of aircraft
that Apollo's maker cast in upward parabolic fall & downward
pilot splayed and child's work his wreck
I walked in '70 the ruined fields above Diana's house the B-17s
departed Hacheston not for German targets but forever
F-16s were flying then from Bent-
waters   river if you trust the scratchings on the nave of
Parham church had been a source of navigable reaches ships of
little draft came all the way from Normandy past
Orford Sloughden Iken down the stream behind her house that
flows into a pipe below a petrol station now
that Aldeburgh programs thanked the US Air Force which had
modified its flight plans and reconnaissance
all for the première of 14 Shostakovich with a dodman on
the Eastern point of Southwold and the
Deben called Adurnus by the Latins on the Alde
all that nearly forty years ago and now a graybeard and
his wife pull up beside the village hall in
Hacheston   waist-high grass and no one come to
shore up crumbling walls it's just
                        the sort of place you . . .

& especially on a cold Christmas when it still was inhabited
by villagers who brought in the harvest
had the local accent
gave me tea and scones beside the wood fires in cottages
frozen to the beams in the OPEC embargo   meant
you'd light your house with candles when electricity
was cut by Ipswich station   only two of us were out that
morning with a low fog and stiff wind off the sea
Mrs Orford pushing on her creaky pram all full of firewood
I knew she'd say *see my pretty baby!* village idiot for sure

my daughters three and five were safe inside their mother's
childhood home   gray smoke from chimney
curling in the sky and through a window of the last house
along the street they called The Street I saw an old woman
cutting up the veg and dropping carrots onions greens
into a pot while in the next room behind her was an even
older man who played the violin   he stopped
and looked out at me while I was looking in   waved
his bow and started up again
I turned my collar up & walked into the wind   I was

7.

happy as I've ever been

                        & saw a need
abiding there and
taking form   it's not from kin in your control
hard to say much more than farm & that   frame
's not to be discounted to
a point it isn't seen or heard   the kettle on the hob
and up upon the pastor hill   cattle
walking in a little word   more than that the hermeneutist all
trigonic as a technicolor splash   hay wain
wainscoting or the rain   haven't much to do with it but still
you might place a neuron unit
                 on an empty cottage's decaying windowsill

and here as part of JM's model of the
cortex if I've overstood (1) your question paperly and
(2) the Damascene converters in your car   so you may pass
the sign and you may miss your turn
it's picturesque and synesthetic on the left and right
Feonic FI Drive
perhaps it's best located in the night

        any surface is a loudspeaker speak
        last in less time it takes to sink an enterprise

        an exitprise

        parse at quick pace and press at will
        brain did it say barn

coda is a Kodak moment meister   clickquack   clack

Sonnet: Send

Dear Bob and Michael: although I'm pretty sure
This book contains a good many typos
And other kinds of carelessness, I'm sending it
Along to you as an attachment.

Please print it out and put it in a safe place.
Sometime or other it may be in a satisfactory
State to publish. Meanwhile it makes me
Feel easier to know that at least two friends

Have a rough copy in their possession.
I had meant to include my usual page or so
Of notes on sources and, as it were,

The *dramatis personae*. Haven't done that yet.
I'll be away for a while, but back in touch
Eventually. Here come the Trigons. Yrs, JM.

Sonnet: Delete

Dear Bob and Michael: although I'm pretty sure
He had something going in the book
He talked with you about and from which you saw
A few lines and passages,

I've decided to delete it from his memory.
Please destroy any pages and/or references
You may have saved. It makes me feel easier
To know there won't be any fragments

Stuck in somebody's computer.
He had meant to spend at least another year
Working on the contradictions,

Punctuation, syntax, overall coherence
And all that. Then he left it as it was. He'll be away
For a while. There go the Trigons. Yrs, JM.

www.ingramcontent.com/pod-product-compliance
Lightning Source LLC
Chambersburg PA
CBHW021327190426
43193CB00039B/415